Poems of my Soul

ISIDOROS KARDERINIS

Poems of my Soul

Translation: MARY SAVVIDOU

ATHENS/GREECE 2014

authorHOUSE®

AuthorHouse™ LLC
1663 Liberty Drive
Bloomington, IN 47403
www.authorhouse.com
Phone: 1-800-839-8640

Published by AuthorHouse 05/09/2014

ISBN: 978-1-4969-1146-9 (sc)
ISBN: 978-1-4969-1118-6 (e)

Library of Congress Control Number: 2014908424

Travelling in the desert

That honey-golden morning
Starting on the tall camels' humps
From the small Bedouin camp
For the vast golden brown desert
And with the gigantic and blazing sun
Burning merciless in the dusty sky
We hardened our souls in the furnace.

We knew we wouldn't find beautiful flowers
Nor trees to cast their shadows upon us.

We knew we wouldn't find crystal flowing fountains
Nor shells rooted in the sand.

We knew we wouldn't find song birds
Nor wind to cool us down.

We knew we wouldn't find sweet eyes
Nor a Siren to sing for us.

We knew we wouldn't find hospitable words
Nor a star to guide us.

We knew we wouldn't find white country chapels
Nor a priest to give us commune.

But nevertheless we were absolutely determined
To search night and day for the oasis.

I don't know tonight

Tonight I don't know what to write about
For the fire that burns in my guts
For the wind that tortures my body
For the line that slashes my fingers.

Tonight I don't know what to paint
The crack that gawps on my face
The rain that bleeds my heart
The darkness that embraces my stare.

Tonight I don't know what to sing
The ballad which reminds me of her figure
The music that washes ashore my tears
The melody that incarnates her touch.

Tonight I don't know where to lay
My dream was washed out by the big wave.

A soul is leaving

When a soul
Flutter in the half dark sky

A piano note full of grief
Drops on the floor.

A white candle
Extinguishes its vivid flame.

A golden watch
Stops its rhythmic beat.

A novel book
Turns its last page.

A song bird
Sings its great sorrow.

A smiling flower
Glum in the flower garden.

A crystal bell
Breaks in a violet sound.

A willowy cypress
Slowly moves on the peaceful hill.

And a bitter tear
Runs down the cheek of twilight.

A trip to Nile

Travelling by the river boat
On the bluish green waters of Nile
Looking at the banks the clusters of canes
And of acacias with their small yellow, spherical shaped flowers
Listening to the hissing of the exotic serpents
Gazing in the valley with the palm trees
A herd of deer
I was turning over the pages of the colourful book that life
Lented me.

And suddenly a strong, erotic wind
Wildly caresses the book and turns the pages
Pushes a bunch of clouds
Rocks the trees from the roots
Rips out the bushy plants
Disturbs the calm waters of the life-giving river
Which, foaming, they crash at the verdurous banks
I feel in my heart the successive beats that love
Generates.

I turn my stare towards the west
A carmine, ripe sun
Plunges its jaws
At the hollows of the facing rocky hill range
A heron crosses the blood-red horizon
Like the scissor that cuts the line
In two pieces
I feel flooded by the untold melancholy that death
Spreads.

Outcast

On the wooden bench
As a rag that stinks
I sleep
The dismal winter nights
With the freezing breeze
That tortures
My cachectic body.

I have nothing
In this unfair world
That I scrape a living
And the cruel sun
As a false coin
From my pierced pocket
Rolls
On the dirty pavement.

I don't have dreams
And my soul has become black
As the hearse
That every morning
Empty
Passes
In front of me
As if it calls me to take me away.

I can't stand it anymore
Life's thorny road
Has deeply hurt me.

Nightmare

Last night
In my dream
I saw the sky
Darkened
Flowing
Carmine blood
Like a fountain
I saw the sun
Sorrowful
Suddenly
Getting black
I saw the streets
Sunk
In the desperation
Of death
I saw the trees
Submerged
In mourning
Wearing
Black bands
On their arms
I saw houses
In ruins
Amongst flames

And smoke
I saw people
Dead
With heads, hands
And legs
Cut out
I saw children
With faces
Full of bruises
Crying woefully
In the rubbles
I saw vultures
Pecking
On the dead bodies
I saw the wind
Carrying
On his shoulders
The stench
Of the rotten
Meat.

I wish it was only that
A nightmare.

Poet

I throw the bucket
In the garden's well.

All around trees
And flowers
Thirsty.

I pull up dreams
That sparkle
In the sun's touch.

And I water with them
Their roots.

The melancholy of loneliness

When the loneliness
With the moth eaten face
And the bony hands
Like a perverse wind
Knocked loudly at my door
The dark sky
Surrounded at once my existence.

Since then the house empty
Doesn't speak to me not even a word
Its walls melancholic and stiff
Don't smile to me at all
The big mirror in the sitting room
Sullen
As a cloud ready to poor down the rain
Got unbearably tired
Looking only at me every day.

But also in the mossy garden
Since many years flowers
Don't bloom
As the spring sun
No longer visible
Doesn't see them
The birds silent
On the withered branches of the trees
Don't sing to me
And the stone fountains
Ceaselessly water my soul
With poisoned water.

The garden with the statues

As I cross
The baluster gate
Of the garden
With the upright statues
In front of me
Are rising
Tall palm trees
With branches
Like the quills of the pens
Unfading red roses
Shed their fragrance
Of immortality
Cool springs
Gushing
Sleepless water
Blue birds
Are crossing the sky.

And the statues
In the clearing
Washed
By the eternal light
Of the sun
With figures
Full of glory
And white eyes
Are staring
Contemplative
The deep horizons.

So, the future
Must be born
Shiny
As a platinum star
Laying
On these
Wise statues.

The erotic song of the sea

Oh, wide sea, tonight I want to sing for you
Your little waves splashing at my heart's seashore
Your love words wet my ears drop by drop
Your silver hair which drip spices I long to touch.

Oh my sweet sea, your lips tonight I want to kiss
Your blue eyes are shinning at the moon's caresses
My dreams as little boats are floating on your tender breasts
Your body's sensual honey let me harvest.

The death of a poet

Under these
Snow-white marbles
The poet lies
His alabaster bones
As if they are alive
Creaking all the time.

The day he died
The sun set early
The birds stopped
Singing their melodies
The sky dressed
The dark veil
Of the big lament
The moon melancholic
Dipped in the black nets
Of silence
The stars forgot
To come out
Of their hiding places
The flowers sullen
Suck
The earth's sobs.
The wind weathered trees
While the piano's
Mournful music
Was folded out,
Tearfully were rustling their leaves
The pages of his books
Paled with sadness.

His verses immortal
Bright sonorous trumpets
Will never cease
Vibrating our souls.

Rummaning the past

Sitting
At the banks of the river
That floats peacefully
I recall
In my memory
The days
That pass meaningless
Like songs
Without rhythm
The words
That went astray
Among the reeds
The tears
That flew in vain
On the cheeks
The expectations
Which were buried
Like the dead man
In the ground
The dreams
That burned out
Like the oil lamp
That has no oil.

I was left like that
An empty shell
Looking at the river.

Tilted frame

Striding over the threshold
Of the ruined mansion
I entered the huge
Dark lounge
Everywhere the empty present
Only on the dirty wall
Next to the half broken fireplace
A frame that tilts
As a ship
On the swelling sea.

At its face
An ancient-like balcony
With a panoramic view
To the endless
Blue sea
A white swallow
That rushes
In the cloudless sky
A cherry table
On it a silver
Relief fruit bowl
With ornamental grapes
Over flown
Like a cup of wine
A golden apple
That sparkles
As the sun touches it
With its fingertips
A porcelain vase
With colourful, blooming
Flowers.

And in its soul
Mournful tears
As wild rivers
For a luminous past
That fainted away
Like the letters
On the fair sand
That wiped away
By the foaming wave.

Come back

Since you're gone the garden is melancholic
The roses faded
The ones that bloomed at the velvet touch of your hands
Grass grew on the words of love
We had exchanged under the sky's starlight.
Yellowish they fell from the tree branches
In the fist wind's autumn blow
The tender feelings
Which we hanged like fresh green leaves.
The passionate kisses got wet
Which like the ripe fruits of our flaming love
We had harvested in the corner of the blooming garden.
On the hardened soil
Spiral brooklets of sub saline water formed
The ivy stopped climbing up the stone wall.

Now your absence like the fire burns the heart
Now your memory as a huge rock
Crashes the breast
Now the distant echo of your voice a sad note
That tortures the inner of the soul.

So let's forget
The cloudy days that nurtured the separation
Those grim days that we walked
On the craggy uphill of grief.

Come back and rise as the fair dawn
With the honey-gold sun on your blue forehead
And dry the humid from the tears soil.

Memory restoration

Tranquil twilight.

In the first note of the piano
The silence
Which the wind has carved
On the precipitous rocks
Is broken
The birds wake up
From the lethargy
In which they had fallen into
The memory
Dazing from the deep sleep
Gets up from its bed
Tottering
And wears the light.
The dead images
Come to life again
Dissolving the fog
That surrounded them.
The petrified sounds
From the channels
Of the past
Sound loudly
The shadowy marbles
Are limed

By the shinning
Of the sky
The withered flowers
That their flame
Has faded
They boost again
The profound ideas
Which watered the foundations
Of the majestic
Structure
Are drawn up
At the sea's surface
By the nets of memory
The wise words
Which were forgotten
Are shinning like stars
The rusted clocks
Inside the dusty drawers
Begin to tick.

In the dull landscape
Of the present
The lighter which was ignited
Like the glow of the sun
Brings back alive
The lost memory.

I complain

I complain
For the ragged children that beg for money at the traffic lights,
For the corpses of life that pierce their veins on the stairs,
For the outcasts of society who are sleeping on the benches.

I complain
For the birds that fly in the lead sky,
For the trees that breath with difficulty in the gardens,
For the passer-bys that throw their garbage on the pavements.

I complain
For the unemployed youth that see their dreams extinguishing,
For the insufficient knowledge they receive in schools,
For the stars which can not bloom in this landscape.

I complain
For the rodents that gnaw at our houses planks,
For the cheap spectacles that drug our minds,
For the big eyes that follow us in the dark.

An emigrant coal miner

The poverty has led me to Belgium' s tunnels
My life now as the light in the candle flickers
The black shadow of Death follows me in my every step
The gun in my soul has opened a huge pit.

My face as the white paper is grimed
My breath is heavy from the hovering coal dust
The unbearable heat roasts my tortured body
I will leave my bones here in the cruel foreign land.

Seaside

On this fascinating seaside
Since the first moment
My eyes got peaceful
Favoured by the fate
Which with its azure playing
Was carving deep inside me
The cool flame
Of a world unbelievably radiant.

And when digging in the blond sand
With suntanned body
A white face eaten by the salt
Suddenly smiled at me
The shovelfuls of sweat that I had shed
Generously they rewarded me.

And close by, the seagulls
Surrendered to their blithe
Flying above the snow white fleece
Of the waves
Like marvellous painters
They drew
With their crows
The rare picturesque beauty of the landscape.

Likewise now
Opening my immense stare
To the deep blue celestial concave
Which has the golden yellow sun
Pinned on its chest
They shiver from the tree of my soul
Like green leaves
A lake of transparent feelings.

At the death's door

I count the pinned stars
At the celestial concave
That flicker as the flame
Of my burned candle
I count the closely written pages
In the book of my memories
That as sad notes
Are scratching my soul
I count the pointless carved steps
In the arena of life
Which fade away as flocks of birds
In the endless horizon.

I count the last hours
Which like blood-cruel hyenas
With sharp teeth and crooked nails
Are getting ready to devour
My sick body.

Abandoned cemetery

Walking in the abandoned cemetery
Gazing at the lean cypresses
That move at the wind's autumn blow
Staring at the broken tombs
With the half erased names
I was recalling the faded images of a past
That's gone

I bend and cut a fistful of wild grass
That sprouts everywhere on the moist ground
A cluster of nettles show me their teeth,
A lizard crawls on the greyish, stone wall
A crow flies around in the half darkened sky
I hear the muffled cries of a future
That comes.

We will all become broken tombs.

Father can you hear me

Father can you hear me
You left
And the sky went dark
The clouds gigantic
Crying they drag
Their steps
The birds don't fly
They hide inside the forests
And the shrubberies
The sun exhausted
Leans on its pillow
The sea black
And sullen
Lost its calmness
The mountains frowning
Got covered with their snow white
Blanket
The meadows joyless
Devitalized
As abandoned
Cemeteries
The rivers over flooded
Got white with anger
The lakes froze
As it did the smile on the lips.

Father can you hear me
You left
And the city turned grey
The roofs emit
Black smoke
The balconies drip
Bitter tears
On the slippery pavements
The streets deserted
In their despair
Surrendered
The chestnut bakers in the corners
Sorrowful
Warm their hands
The statues in the squares
Naked
Trembling in the cold
The gardens melancholic
With wind weathered trees
Bending
In the blackened sky

Father can you hear me
You left
And on the pain's breasts
Eternally pecking
The lammergeyer.

The shirt of society

The silken shirt of society
Unfortunately has many spots.

The Islands of the Aegean Sea

These islands which the Aegean Sea holds tight in its cool embrace
Were made of soaked-sea stone and golden sun.

The east's bells rang blissfully in the dawning sky
And the wind with its transparent hands
laid laurels and olive tree leaves.

The schooners embroidered with golden threads the seashores
And the elaborated craftsmen built white houses with blue windows.

The waves carved smiling faces with their white saltiness
And the seagulls with their wings painted the beauty of the landscape.

The brown mountains jammed between their
brows the small country churches
And the few trees honeyed with a green tone their naked heart.

The spades dug the earthen bowels of the barren land
And marble statues came out in the light with history's sweet talking.

On these steep rocks blooming flowers grew
Which decorated with grace Greece's blue-white hair.

⁓•⁓

Years of childhood in poverty

I remember the poverty years
That I lived when I was a child.

The mended clothes
That I wore everyday to school.

The shoes with the holes
That filled with mud when it rained.

The little box with which
I painted the other people's shoes.

The meagre food
That barely let me survive.

The cachectic geranium
In the broken tile pot.

Our low ceiling home
That sun couldn't reach at dawn.

And the grandmother
In the frozen nights of winter
Near the grey burning wood stove
Filling me with dreams
As she read to me fairytales.

But when the fairytales ended
The raw reality began.

You came

Since early in the morning the snow falls heavily
On my stuffed garden the snow is already laid
The trees wear their white clothes
And my breath has blurred the window pane.

The sparrows roosted in their nests
The cats stopped their meows
The creation around, melancholic, is crystallized
And our city's streets have emptied.

Despite all these you managed to come
And you brought in to my frozen heart the spring
Holding in one hand bloomed flowers
And on the other dew-filled songs.

Unemployment

One year now the darkness of unemployment covers me
Now I feel as a thrown cigarette on the street
The burden of life is heavy on my tired shoulder
And my tormented heart aches and sighs.

My minor children are lacking even the bread
My wife inside our cold home desperate and pale
The debts have overrun us, as a winter rain
Oh, society, how unfair you really are and cruel.

Flash

In the winter flashes
The lead sky
As the flash
In the camera
Capturing
In the passing time
The absences of the future.

Born deaf

I never heard
The cries of the birth's aches
The rustling of the leaves
The whinny of the horse
The bell's rings
The nightingale's song.

I never heard
The wind's whistling
The plashing of the waves
The clank of the thunderbolts
The sound of the piano
The rain's song.

I never heard
The echo of my voice
I was born out from the guts
Of the silence.

Newborn

In his cradle submerged
He just opened his eyes
He just touched the world
He just smelled the wind
He just heard the rain
He just tasted the sun.

He came to live his lie too.

Prophet of bad news

I see the sun pale
In the sky's bed.

I see the sea sick
Burning with fever.

I see the mountains ill
Spilling blood on their handkerchiefs.

I see the trees scrubby
Loosing their hair.

I see the birds dizzy
Staggering as they fly.

I see black clouds
As the lines of the palm
Telling our unfair fate.

Two rings

Two rings
Life
Has given me.

A white
And a black.

The white
Full of light
Rejoice
My eyes.

The black
Full of darkness
Hurts
My soul.

Reader

I read the books
That writhe at my touch
Their pages
Full of lines
That mirror their soul.

In them I found the light.

———•———

Lost sun

The sun that burns in the sky
Belongs equally to everyone.

But there are people
That have never seen it.

The melancholic man

I love
The lead sky
The rain that seeps in my heart
The wet figures in the sullen streets
The grey trees in the boring yards
The roofs that dip in the clouds
The sad music of the piano.

I love
The wind that sweeps my inner soul.

Bleeding verses

I have read
Many great verses.

But I will never forget
The verses
Of the freedom fighter
That were written in his blood
On his cell's walls.

Expectation of death

Inconceivable it hurts
The expectation of death.

Lucky those
Who die suddenly.

The girl of the sea

You hung the sun with its flaming mane
As a golden pendant on your rose neck
And you blinded my eyes girl of the sea.

You were singing melodic love verses
In the summer's crystal heat
And as a Siren you sweetened my ears.

You lay with the beautiful lines of your body
Naked on the noon's hot sand
And you set on fire the desires in my eyes.

You were waving your golden brown hair
As you were walking on the white waves
And their breeze was cooling my heart.

Beggar

On the dirty pavement
Since the dawn I'm sitting down
As a garbage thrown away
I seek a few crumbs
From the sky's bread
I seek an open flower
From the heart's gardens
I seek a sweet smile
From the sun's lips.

I seek a compassion gaze
From Madonna's eyes.

A rebel and two executioners

The rebel
Chained in his cell
And the brutal executioners
Are preparing the whips.

Then one of them asks:
"Where shall we start?"

And the other:
"Leave the body.
His mind has points
Let's make it smooth."

Hero

Fighting for ideals
He spilled his blood.

And the sun that didn't forget him
Unfolded its wings
And embraced him in eternity.

Fragile life

Our life is so fragile
That can break in a moment
As a flowery glass vase.

Alone in front the fireplace

Alone in front the marble fireplace
With its wild flame tongues
Licking my bluish eyes
I remember the efflorescent rose days
We lived together as swallows in love.

Those days that was warming me
The flaming breath of your body
The flaming sunbeams of your hair
The radiant caress of your eyes
The velvet kiss of your lips
The sensual touch of your hands
The steamed flowers of your heart.

Now although the living room is comfortably hot
My heart is shivering frozen
As the fallen white snow outside.

The river's water

I took the water from the restless river's blue body
And I drunk it under the old plane tree's the cool shadow
The plane's leaves were rustling in the dawn's serene colour
And from the opposite golden-honey mountains, wings were jumping.

My spirit was touched softly by the sun's golden rays
And my rising soul slowly was painted by the light
My body was hugged by the green fibers of the flowers
And by the wind's windbags the weather was poured in abundance.

My roots green, were moving in the brown fruitful soil
And the blood was flowing, writhing in the vessel's openings
The dark clouds had not come out on the stolid sky yet
And the crackles stones were founded with labour from yesterday.

The ideals were shinning as the sky's un-extinguished flame
And the birds' chirpings were scattering redundant fragrance
The juices were running from the amber grape
And the dreams were moving straight with imperious walking.

The prisoner's ballad

When I crossed
The doorstep of the underground prison
It was a glumly sunset
The darkness thick
Like a spider it was weaving in my eyes
A huge net
And as the brutal prison guard
Unlocked the door of my cell
With an awful sound
The tears of my black soul
As a waterfall were running
On the dirty ground.

My days
Were passing in a slow pace
In sorrow and wailing
I didn't see her serene face
Who was erased
With the heavy iron door's sound
I didn't hear her sweet words
That as yellow leaves
Had fallen on the frozen soil
My heart now alone
As a forest in flames was burning
From the great longing.

The walls of my cell were dirty
Without even a small window
And as the worm
On the ground I was crawling
With my disgusting body
And when I dared
A cry of despair to shout
They tortured me for hours naked
With a thorny whip
I was praying to God for death
For salvation
From this horrible torture.

But no one heard me
And in my wounded guts
Day by day the bad thing was growing big
My bloody hands
Were throwing nettles
My bitter tongue
By the thirst and the hunger dominated
Was dipping a river of poison
Not been able to hold any longer
In this hell
I started using drugs
To live an illusory dream.

And a grey dawn
That they had me chained
In the dark yard
I saw a man in the Death Row
Passing by, escorted
With a cloud on the deathlike forehead
And the executioner waiting on the scaffolding
To put around his neck
The tight loop
For he had to pay for the hideous murder
He committed the day of Christmas
Without any hesitation.

And when finally
After so many sad years
The big day came
From the pitch dark
And this stinky prison
That as mice
The prisoners are held
To get released
With unsaid yearning
I was waiting
To see her brown eyes
But also a piece of blue sky.

The ship of slaves

In the rotten slavery ship
As lifeless sardines loaded
We look for a piece of hope
In a land we were not born there.

The waves gigantic and foaming
They constantly fight to drown us
But the merciful God don't want
The ocean's fishes to eat us.

And when in the lonely, foreign port
The rotten ship at last arrives
Unbearable hardship again awaits us
When the heartless sun will turn rose?

Katmandu

It was September of the Cross
And the blue sea was calm
Our ship in Lima of Peru
And a seagull on the mast rope.

At his right hand he had a tattoo
And he smoked with pleasure his pipe
His name was Ari Karmandu
And he had his curly hair parted.

His country was Mauritania
And he was a sailor for thirty four years
His wife's name was Maria
And he met her at Bologna.

When his shift on the ship was over
And the stars were dancing in the sky
He went to the stern with a book
And he read it enthusiastically.

He sharpened his mind with the knife
His net at the bottom of the sea
And me, the untrained, I learned much
By my wise friend Katmandu.

The slogan

They wrote the slogan on the wall and left
Then the rain came down and erased it
But they went and wrote it again
Finally their persistence won.

Marked cards

On the round
Table
With the black
Baize
I play koltsina
With Death.

The cards
Masterly
Marked
By him.

The game
I have it
In advance
Lost.

———•———

We planted

We planted our seeds in the clouds
And instead of roses the rain germinated.

We planted our footprints on the sand
And instead of light the sun burned us.

We planted our dreams in the sea
And instead of peace the waves drifted us away.

Eternal marbles

These white marbles
Were created by the light of the sun.

In their relief veins
The pulse of eons beats.

The shoulders of the rock
Are sinking by the inconceivable weight.

Only the wise ones are carrying them.

The sweet dawn of poetry

In the earthly city the sweet dawn rises
And the poet who woken up early
In the desk of his house
Writes verses.

Poetry does not change the world
But as the sun's light
In the smiling dawn sky
Illuminates the consciousness.

The house by the seashore

That house by the seashore
With the blue windows
That the winds whiten
Longs for my footsteps.

Inside the garden the father's voice
The goldfinches on the tree branches
The summers here were unforgettable
And my heart bleeds.

The plucking

I remember when we were kids
In our carelessness
We were plucking margaritas.

Now, in life's hole
We are plucking the nights with moon.

A road with three buildings

In the road's beginning a new building
Bathed by the sun's golden rays.

In the middle of the road a worn building
Damaged by the time's touch.

In the end of the road a skeleton building
Drown in a black cloud.

The mystery of life

No matter how much I searched the illuminated
sky, I couldn't find not even a star
To light the unsolved mystery of the universal life.

———•———

Come and dissipate the fog

Outside the big Glasgow port in Scotland
Our ship in the deep fog is lost
Its grey horn hoarsely blows continuously
And I, standing on the ship's bridge I long for you to come.

I want you to wear that nice blue dress
And the gold pendant I bought in Marseilles
And as a fairy, light, fresh and sweet
My melancholic heart to heal tonight.

A small ship

A small ship desperate
In the black seashore
And a pale moon lost
In the sky's clouds.

A bent pine on the uphill
A few grey seabirds
At the window a beautiful daughter
And I, in the company of Plaids.

A small ship plagued
By the weather's bad mood
And a stripped dolphin washed up
In the sea's embrace.

A purple flower in the flower bed
A few leaves fallen on the ground
A cold hand of the North wind
And plenty teardrops shed.

A small ship broken
At the sharp, precipitous rocks
My face wind weathered
And my heart in million pieces.

The old man and his wife

In the old fashioned living room of his house
The old man reads his newspaper
He understands
"The news are fewer as the time goes by"
His wife knits a wool jacket
"A bad winter will come" she thinks.

And their cat indifferently
Plays with the worn ball of life.

Poor pawn

The knee deep in the mud sunk
And the wind wild blowing
The moon in the gorge broken
And my soul alone is gasping.

The firs covered by snow
And the sky pitch black
On the chess board a poor pawn
And the dreams thrown in the river.

The wolves at the summit threatening me
And the leeches sucking my blood
By the thick clouds crows rush down
And at once the lie ends.

Dark life

The silver stars sad
Flaming tears are dropping
Our rose dreams are soaked
And the nightingales sigh.

The golden laughter of the dawn is late
And the wild waves are bubbling
Oh, you are full of darkness, life
And our souls are torn to pieces.

Midnight

Midnight and my heart aches
I was scratched by the nail of the moon

Midnight and my soul writhes
I was stabbed by a star cluster.

Midnight and my wound rages
I was bit by a meteor piece.

Oh, how can I forget

Oh, how can I forget that day
The sea's tender rocking
The sun's golden rustling
But also the sky's peace.

Oh, how can I forget that day
The seashore's flaming golden flower
The cicada's sweet song
But also the wind's gleefulness.

Oh, how can I forget that day
The seagulls' painted flying
The white ships' crossing
But also the dawn's fountain.

Oh, how can I forget that day
The bright stare of her eyes
The drops of dew of her kisses,
But also her body's charming.

The sun's bleeding

The sun bleeds in the sky's body
And the life-giving light more and more dims
The flower of my soul a motionless corpse
And the weather turbulent and mean.

The sea froths continuously with rage
And the ships staggering drunken
The veil of my heart pitch black
And the seagulls for days now gone.

In the desolate seashore the wind rushes
And the trees tortured in desperation
The star of my dream now dies out
And the leaves fall down yellowed.

The beginning of the fairytale

The fairytale unfolds as a ball of threads on the floor
The smiling sun with its golden mane rises
The blue sky lights the soul's countless depths
And the sea's cool breeze carries million passions.

The seagulls are flying around the masts
The waves caress tenderly the shore's golden hair
The chick's eyes are opening and see million colours
And by the guts of the cave rushes a honey perfume.

By the vine's leaves the joy's white tears are dropping
The crystal bells of the dawn are blooming as roses
The statues are standing lofty at the edge of the sour cherry garden
And words green, are rising from the stars' mouth.

Gloomy valley

In the valley of my heart
The sun forgot to rise.

The evening primroses
Opened their dark flowers.

The grass withered
By the gloom's desperation.

The livestock don't graze any more
In deep sleep they are.

The wind's roar brake with pain
At the adjacent hills.

And the bats gigantic
Feed with dead love.

I know a city

I know a city
Where the drums
Beat mournfully.

I know a city
That weaves
In its loom
The darkness.

I know a city
Sank in sadness
That doesn't dreams.

I know a city
That its heart
By the spear poked
Pours blood.

The murder of the moon

I remember with sorrow that it was a dampened, spring night
The soldiers were patrolling the streets with their guns at hand
The clouds battered were hanging by the sky's balcony
The wind, melancholic, was singing in low voice a dead march
The leaves of the trees, yellow, were falling down as if it was autumn
The rain's water as red rivulets was flowing in the drains.

Then I learned that somebody had murdered the silver moon.

The Copenhagen mermaid

I approached the petite, beautiful mermaid
That sits on the rock at the Copenhagen harbor
One white day of the Scandinavian winter
That thick snow was falling by the sky's ceiling.

Her body naked was shaking in the cold
But it was as a statue coming out of the museum
The bells of my heart rung at once
Since I've fallen in love at first sight with her.

The warmth of love

By the sky's grip a star slipped
And it was bitter cold and it was noon.

The passers frozen on the pavements were walking
And the tree branches were trembling and shaking.

But we, holding each other at the street's wet corner
We were burning by the warmth of love.

Poor neighbourhood

The little houses of the poor neighbourhood
are stone made and low roofed
The life giving sun is nowhere to be seen from the dirty, soil alleys
Faces scared by the every day's honest labour
And dusty shoes in the noon's cloudiness.

In the pots the hyacinths are thirsty for cool water
And the window shutters clanking by the wind's longing
Dreams that fade away like the black smoke from the chimney
And pale children flying in the wounded sky.

The heart of the poet

The snow white swallows are flying in the sapphire sky
And the sun with its golden bells is singing.

The flowers are moving slowly as the breeze touches them
And the children are playing in the field's openness.

The crystal water of the fountain is rustling in the cistern
And a deer feeling hot drinks greedy and quenches its thirst.

Then a camellia blooms in the lyric heart of the poet
And its perfume floods the grassy soil.

Fight against the destiny

I was covered by the wild waves of the sea
Now I fight to grab myself from the wings of the seagull.

I was flooded by the funereal sound of the violets
Now I seek the fragrance of the white lily.

I was crushed down by the heavy shadow of the sycamore
Now I seek a sun's golden yellow ray.

I see

I see our wagon in the twilight flopping
The horses scrawny
Floundering on the steep uphill
The beggars on the dirty pavements
Throwing thorns from their fists.

I see the flowers
In the pots on the balconies
Withering in the touch of the foul wind
The window shutters rotting from the rain
The slogans fading away on the walls.

I see the silver light of the lamp posts
Day by day getting dangerously dimmer
The squares orphanated without their statues
The street sweepers joyless
Sweeping uncountable tons of garbage.

Where to look at
So our eyes will not sullen at once?

Lost parrot

In the broad streets of the vast city
I look for a parrot I have lost.

The words that spouted from his beak
Made the curved branches of my soul bloom.

Now I don't hear its human voice
The buzzing of the cars has now covered it.

And the flashing rod of the summer sun
Beats merciless my dark skinned body.

A half ruined tower

A stone half ruined tower
In the golden green field it stands
It recollects the adamant glories it had lived
And in its cloud covered heart it rains.

The lords that once lived there
A life like a fairytale
As the plane tree's leaves have scattered in the wind
And their bones turned to pitch black gravels.

You are away

The stone fireplace in the corner burns
And the deep red flames are vibrant
The huge living room is hot
But my poor heart is cold.

You are away since a month now
And the thick snow has piled
In our home not even a sun's ray
Our love is now extinguished.

The windowpanes are fogged
By the cold winter's breath
The little sparrow on the branch frozen
And in the white garden a turtle.

You are away since a month now
And your absence hurts a lot
The silk thread that held a true love
Is now broken

By the riverside

By the riverside with my eyes wet and gloomy
I met an old wise man who was fishing carelessly.

When I approached him with heavy and tired footsteps
He said to me in his hoarse voice:

"My friend
Don't look at the aglow sun, melancholic and sad
Don't look at the fragrant flowers in the valley, withered
Don't look at the vast blue sea, turbulent
Live as if you were going to die the next second."

The young men of fire

They are brave in the pitch dark mayhem
Their breasts light a vigorous flame
In their lips they smoke heavy cigarettes
Their heart blooms as the lemon tree.

By their forehead spouts the sun's light
In their arms rests the homeland
In their voices all the people vibrate
Their soul, an untitled boat in the storm.

In their hands they hold a melodic guitar
Their hair are messed up by the bad wind
They write slogans on the dirty walls
Their eyes do not wimp by the dreadful death

The coming of love

The golden yellow rays of the sun
Dissolved the web covered pitch black darkness
My sleepless soul overflows
As an overflown wild river
The flaming song of love
Bloomed in the blue lips of the dawn
And a red dove brought me
The letter that I waited for years.

The flowers in the cool garden
Scattered around their warm smiles
The dreams sweetly spurted
Through the sun bathed grass
The babbling water flew melodically
By the cool stone springs
And in my miserable heart
At once the open wounds closed.

Tonight I hid

Tonight I hid in the clouds
And I became dark rain
The birds were pocking my heart
And the grey environment damp.

The tears were flowing to the ground
And the rivulets were moving as snakes
The flowers didn't have colour any more
And the wind was screaming the same.

Tonight I hid inside the guitar
And I became a melancholic tune
Outside vacuous coldness
And the strings were ripping my body.

The lights were blinking wounded
And the words sad and dull
The laughter like the stars is gone
In the pain's dirty hands.

Tonight I hid in the attic
And I became motionless despair
My soul a black steam from the sieve
There is no cure for me.

The return of the immigrant

He knelt with devotion and kissed his country's sacred soil
As a migratory bird he was away for fifty years
in the heartless foreign country
Then he looked at the facing naked
mountains that were still shinning
And a blooming flower spouted in his aching heart.

He was greatly longing for the family, stone house to stare upon
That had in its garden a deep well and climbing jasmines
But also to walk in the poor neighborhood with the dirty roads
Just to remember when he was playing
pentovola with the other children.

He wanted to visit in the cemetery the tombs of his parents
That were shadowed by tall cypresses so he
can leave some purple flowers
Now that he was in the sunset of his tortured eyes,
And beg them to accept him in their warm embrace.

At the street's corner

Alone at the grey street corner
With the cigarette lit on the hand
I long so much for you to come
And the clouds are ready to rain.

The harbor's lights are flickering
And the houses dark and sleepy
The trees in the parks drink tears
And the leaves are falling in desperation.

Alone at the grey street corner
With my wrinkled face wind weathered
I look at the damp golden watch
And the agony slowly moves in my mind.

The harbor's lighthouses are flashing
And the seagulls are nesting frozen
The ships in the dock are shedding tears
And the waves are bursting with anger.

Alone at the grey street corner
With the heart screaming with pain
Since I see you nowhere my Argiro
And as the candle in the Epitaph I melt.

In the nets of my embrace

Your unbraided hair are carried by the wind
At your voluptuous breasts two big apples are standing
Your moon eyes are shinning this afternoon
That from the trees the autumn leaves are falling.

My heart when it sees you as an unwind clock beats
From my black beard yellow sparrows are flying
A strong rain rushes down from the black clouds
That brings you in my warm embrace's nets.

A child was looking at the stars

It was a summer night and a small child was looking at the stars
The red roses in the garden opened their hearts
Happy words traveled to the still untaken castles
And the mandolins scattered their singing perfume.

The pomegranates filled with sweet sounds in their green leaves
The cicadas began dancing on their festive branches
The moon wore its silver in the sky's luminous dome
And the dreams surged with their huge, snow white wings.

Athens

Oh, created by the wisdom hands, fine marbled Athens
The Parthenon a laurel wreath at the Acropolis' rock
Opposite the imperious pyramid hill of Lycabettus
And at Plakas' narrow streets the lilies' perfume.

At Syntagma square the Parliament imposing
And the Tsolias at the Unknown Soldier monument
The Conservatory of Herodes Atticus a marvelous building
And at your heart the fist flame of Democracy.

At the historical Thission of Hephaestus the resplendent temple
And the sun golden at the sky's sapphire body
White shallows are flying high, the bringers of spring
And a painter stands in front of the chamber of Caryatids.

By Adrian's Gate rushes the wind full of colours
And at the Zappion garden the trees sweetly embrace each other
Your sown monuments are floating in the dawn's light
Oh, you, Mistress of the biggest ancient civilisation.

The lake's island

On the blue lake with the white swans
Reflects the silver moon's embrace.

I take the empty boat and slowly move the paddles
The stars are shinning in the sky's silence.

I want to reach the lake's green island
That years now longs for me and calls me.

The birds are flying in the peaceful wind
And at the banks the trees sweetly play the flute.

As I step my foot on the damp land
I hear rustling inside me my generation's voice.

The beauty of the landscape emerges as a painting
And my heart beats loudly and at once it blooms.

The pot with the roses

The pot with the white roses
Fell by the ledge of the world.

The evil hand that pushed it
Didn't repent for its action.

But the sea spread its nets
Affectionately and the pot did not broke.

A gray swallow

In the park alone a gray swallow
The leaves pale are trembling on the branches
The flowers covered by snow
And around excess coldness.

The sky in the black clouds
The wind wild scatters white dust
The feelings in the bad weather
And its heart alone it withers.

Spring

Spring
A poppy blooms in the revived fields
Swallow tails in the mud-made nests
A humming hive on the gardens' flowers
A colourful pallet of an excellent painter
The flying of love in the open hearts
Intoxicating fragrances in the ornate neighborhoods.

And I, inside the fragrance that I longed.

Roses in the ashes

Today is falling a wild, ashen rain
On the city's roses.

The guitars are not singing any more
The waves, rotten, beat the seashore.

Day by day the stamina melts
That nests in their pure soul.

The hearse

It's getting dark
And my heart heavy
Sighs.

At the end of the road
A shinning black hearse
Is waiting for me.

The driver of death
Pushing the crow-horn
Insistently calls me.

But I don't want to enter.

Acrobatics

In the circus
The acrobat
Levitates
His life
The rope
Trembles
At his every
Step
The viewers
Are clapping
The danger.

And I
In the clouds
That are pregnant
With the fearful
Tomorrow.

Autumn

Autumn
A ripe pomegranate in the thorny wind's branches
An awakening inside the lead clouds of the lightning
The soil damp by the sky's crying
Trees naked from their fluffy cape
Yellow fallen leaves like my dreams
Melancholic streets that slip in the past.

And me, in the sorrow that surrounded me.

Torn in to pieces

In my guts the sea moans in anger
And my heart as a windswept ship it tilts.

From the red coloured rocks of the treeless cape
The fire runs and melts my shaggy chest.

The shinny stars continuously falling as bitter gravels
In the pitch black hole of my soul.

The sky froths from its pain as a rabid dog
And bites my tortured face.

A sadistic vulture grabs with its crooked nails
A dead meat and fades away in the inky horizon.

Harmonium music

As the wind pushes
With its fingertips
The harmonium's clavier
Melodic sounds unfold
The stars dance a waltz
In the bright summer sky
The trees and the plants
Revived
In the enchanted gardens
The drunken sea
Begins its song
The fishing boats
In their dizziness
Dream to catch
Beautiful mermaids
In their nets.

And the boys and girls
With hearts honeyed
By the sweet notes
Are kissing passionately
Under to moon's
Silver stare.

My sun

My sun
Every golden dawn
With your bright rays
You paint
The sea's eyelids
The ridges of the mountains
The trees' hair
The lips of the plants.

But also my soul's
Gargle water.

Progressive ideas

As the charcoals
They were thrown
To the heated
Brassier
The profound
Progressive
Ideas.

And the embers
That remained
Were scattered
To the four
Horizons.

Tell me when

Tell me
When the day will awake in the peaceful water
When the sun will smile in the spotless sky
When the wind will stop the awful lamentation.

Tell me
When the earth will celebrate the eternal redemption.

A nautical dream

I remember when I was still a pure school boy
I wanted to be a captain in the seagoing ships
To distant, exotic lands to travel
And the rough seas to tame.

And when after many years I put on the uniform
The joy was overflowing as a spring from my eyes
That as a newborn star my child dream
that I was nurturing in my heart
Took flesh and bones.